EASY GUITAR
WITH NOTES & TAB

CHRIS TOMLIN
see the morning

T0087869

CONTENTS

ISBN-13: 978-1-4234-2676-9
ISBN-10: 1-4234-2676-2

HAL•LEONARD®
CORPORATION
7777 W. BLUEMOUND RD. P.O. BOX 13819 MILWAUKEE, WI 53213

STRUM AND PICK PATTERNS

This chart contains the suggested strum and pick patterns that are referred to by number at the beginning of each song in this book. The symbols ⊓ and ∨ in the strum patterns refer to down and up strokes, respectively. The letters in the pick patterns indicate which right-hand fingers plays which strings.

p = thumb
i = index finger
m = middle finger
a = ring finger

For example; Pick Pattern 2
is played: thumb - index - middle - ring

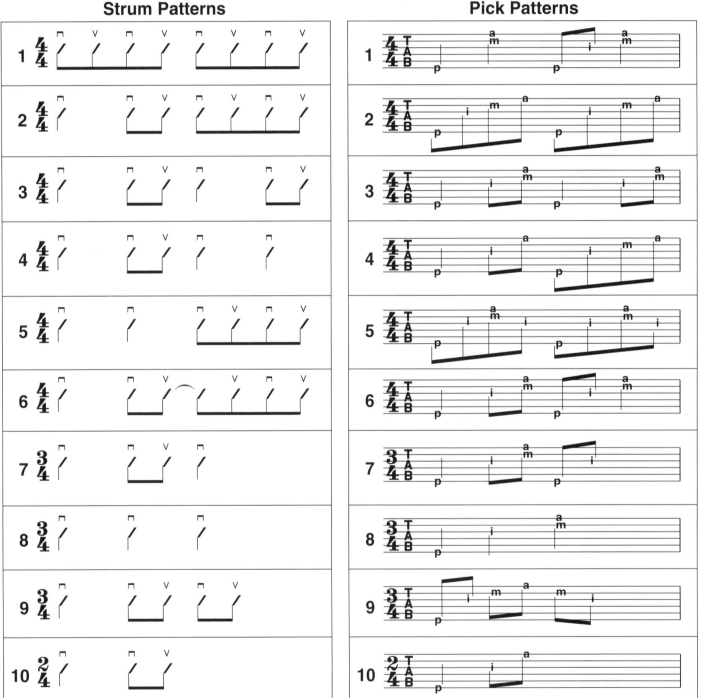

You can use the 3/4 Strum or Pick Patterns in songs written in compound meter (6/8, 9/8, 12/8, etc.). For example, you can accompany a song in 6/8 by playing the 3/4 pattern twice in each measure. The 4/4 Strum and Pick Patterns can be used for songs written in cut time (¢) by doubling the note time values in the patterns. Each pattern would therefore last two measures in cut time.

Made to Worship

Words and Music by Chris Tomlin, Ed Cash, and Stephan Sharp

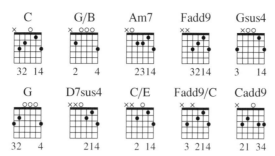

Strum Pattern: 3, 4
Pick Pattern: 4, 5

Verse
Moderately

1. Be - fore the day, _ be - fore the light, _ be - fore the world _ re -
2. All we are _ and all we have _ is all a gift _ from

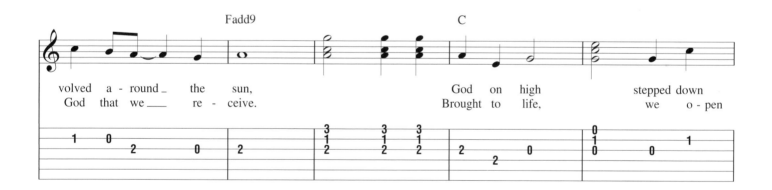

volved a - round _ the sun, God on high stepped down
God that we _ re - ceive. Brought to life, we o - pen

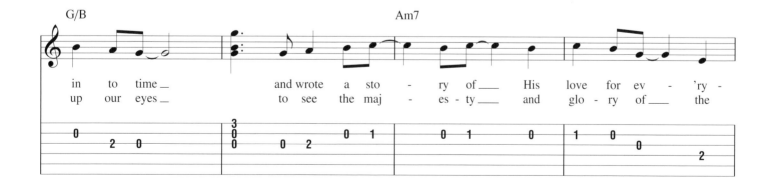

in - to time _ and wrote a sto - ry of _ His love for ev - 'ry -
up our eyes _ to see the maj - es - ty _ and glo - ry of _ the

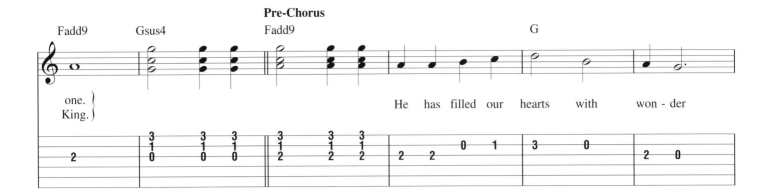

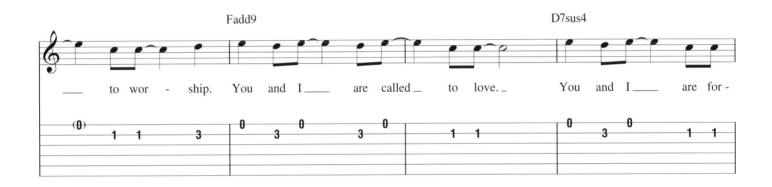

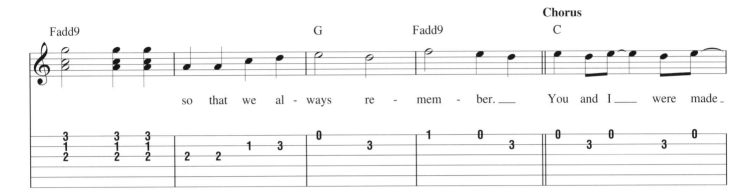

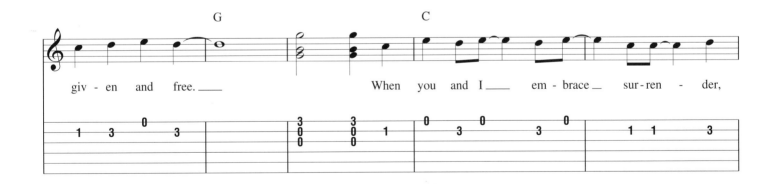

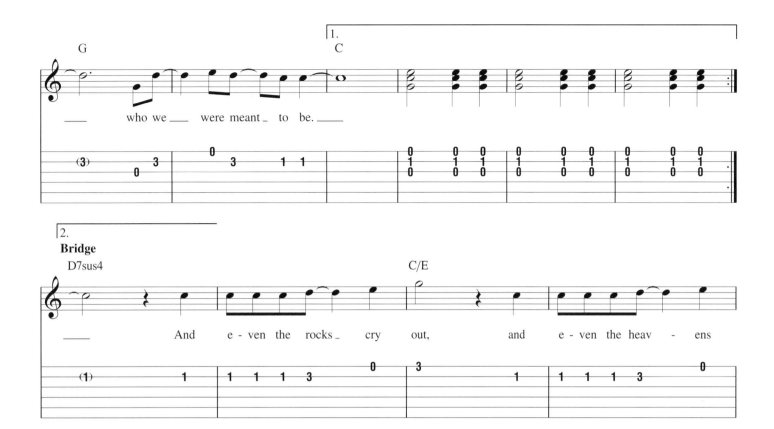

who we ___ were meant ___ to be. ___

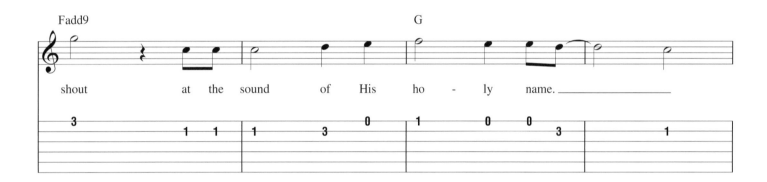

And e - ven the rocks ___ cry out, and e - ven the heav - ens

shout at the sound of His ho - ly name. _____

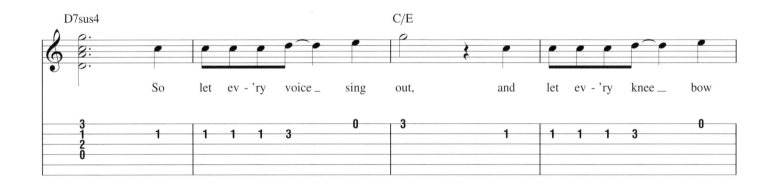

So let ev - 'ry voice ___ sing out, and let ev - 'ry knee ___ bow

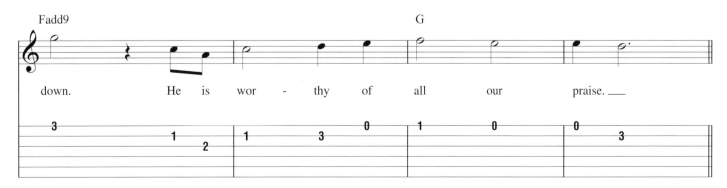

down. He is wor - thy of all our praise. ___

Chorus

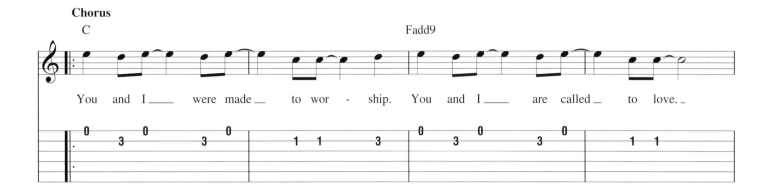

C   Fadd9

You and I ___ were made ___ to wor - ship. You and I ___ are called ___ to love. ___

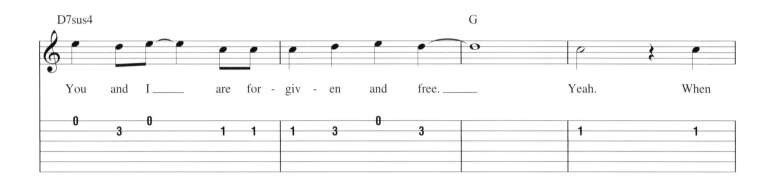

D7sus4   G

You and I ___ are for - giv - en and free. ___ Yeah. When

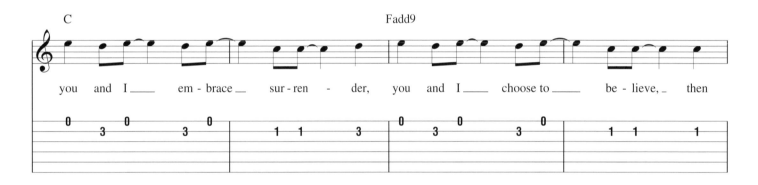

C   Fadd9

you and I ___ em - brace ___ sur - ren - der, you and I ___ choose to ___ be - lieve, ___ then

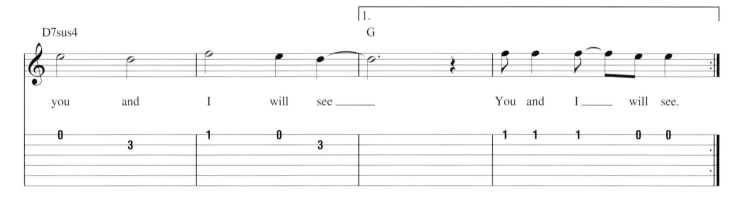

|1.

D7sus4   G

you and I will see ___ You and I ___ will see.

|2.

Outro

G   C

___ who we ___ were meant ___ to be. ___ Yeah, ___

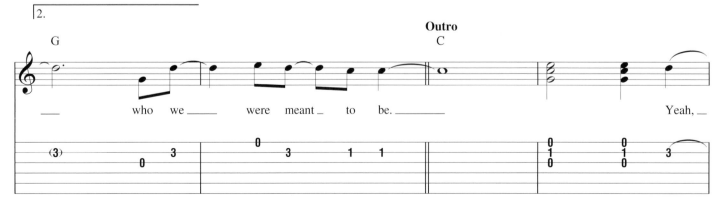

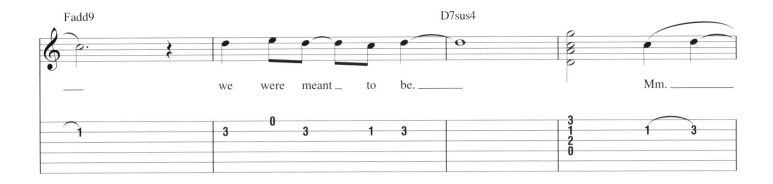

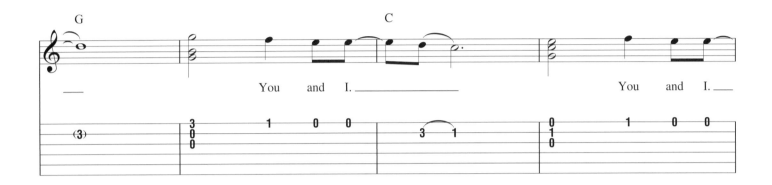

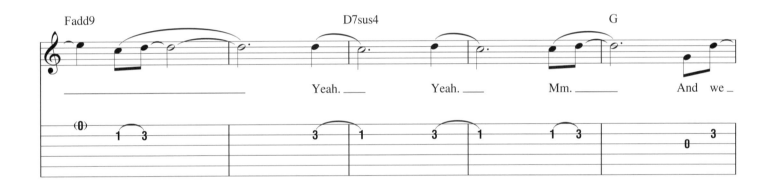

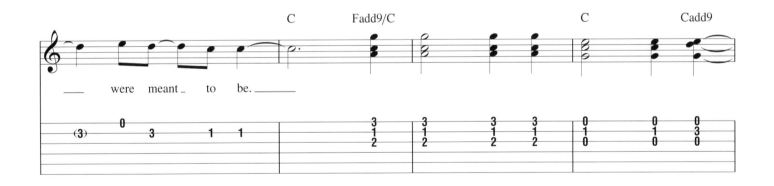

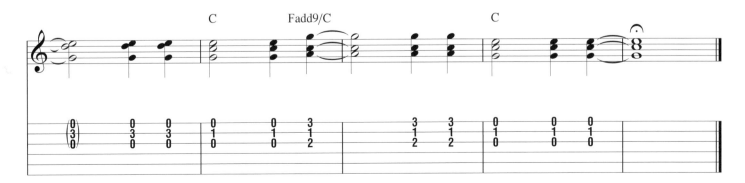

How Can I Keep from Singing

Words and Music by Chris Tomlin, Matt Redman and Ed Cash

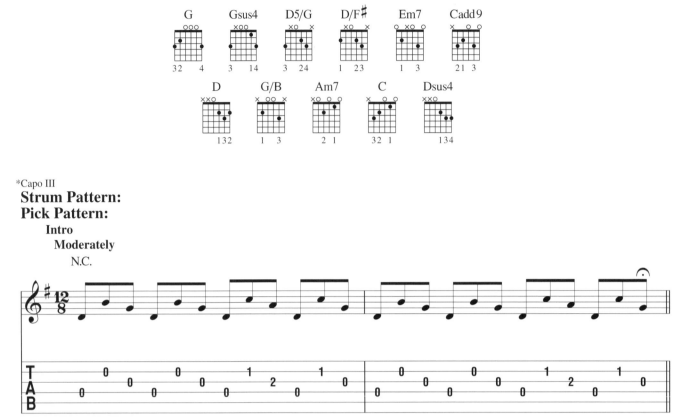

*Capo III

Strum Pattern:
Pick Pattern:

Intro
Moderately
N.C.

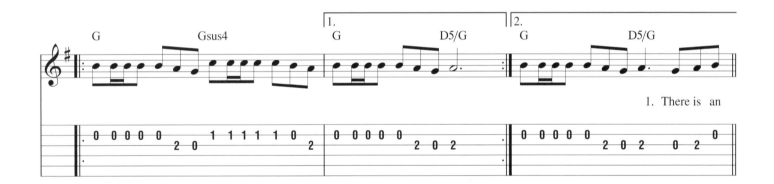

*Optional: To match recording, place capo at 3rd fret.

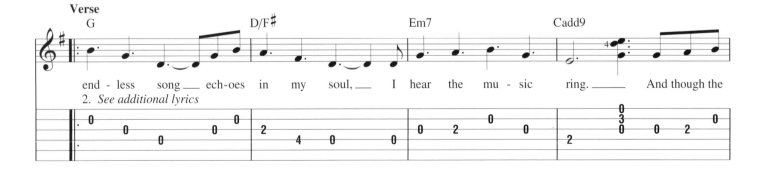

end-less song ech-oes in my soul, I hear the mu-sic ring. And though the

2. See additional lyrics

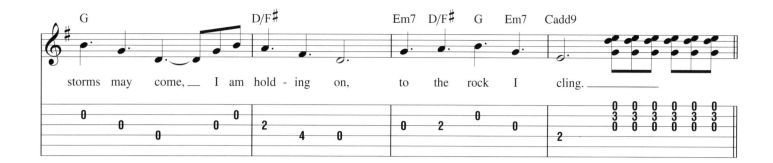

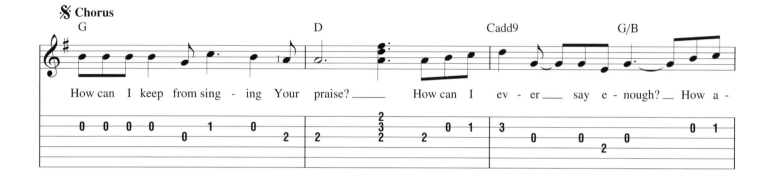

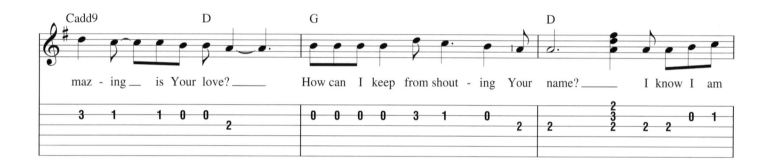

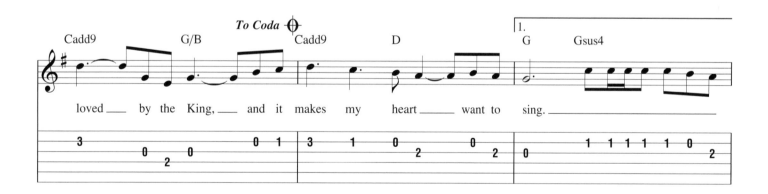

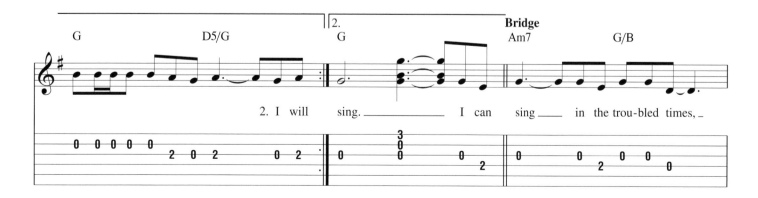

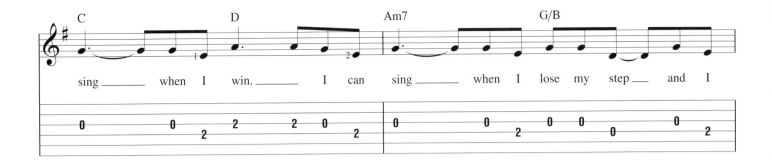

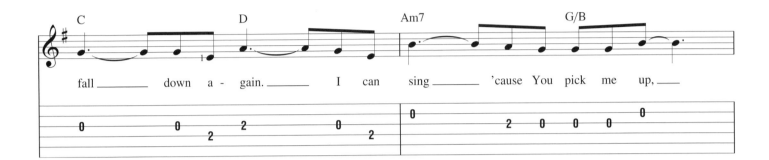

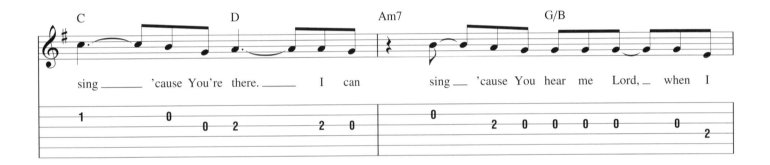

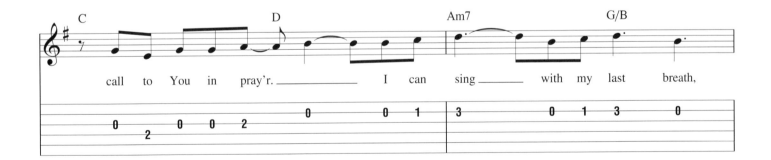

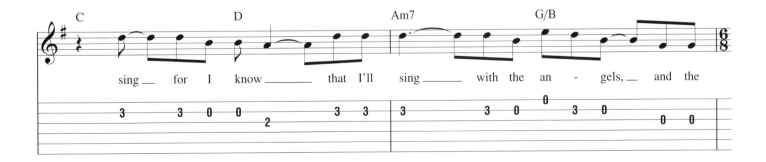

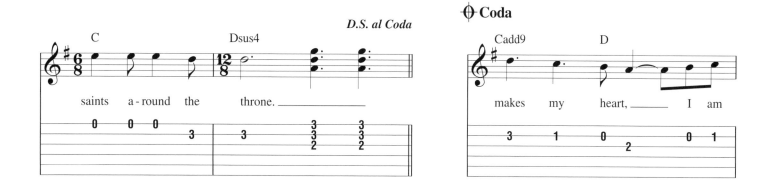

D.S. al Coda

⊕ **Coda**

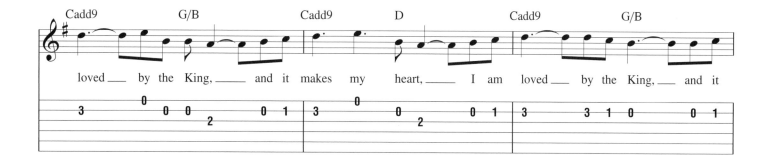

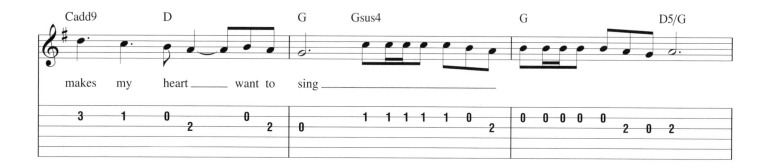

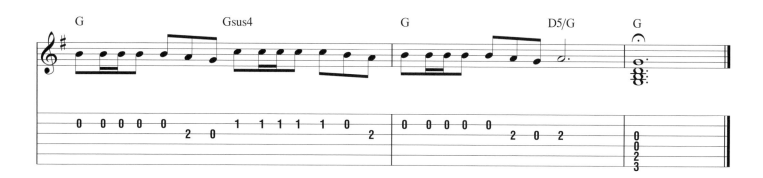

Additional Lyrics

2. I will lift my eyes in the darkest night,
   For I know my Savior lives.
   And I will walk with You knowing You see my through,
   And sing the songs You give.

Let God Arise

Words and Music by Chris Tomlin, Jesse Reeves and Ed Cash

*Optional: To match recording, place capo at 2nd fret.

Pre-Chorus

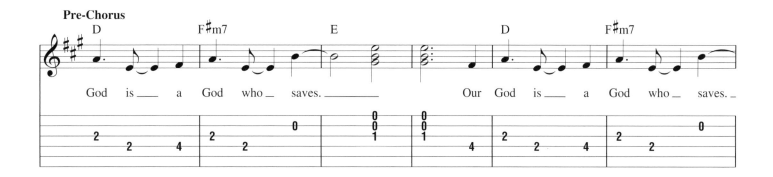

God is ___ a God who ___ saves. _____ Our God is ___ a God who ___ saves. ___

𝄋 **Chorus**

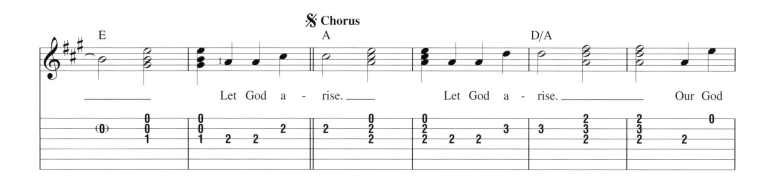

_____ Let God a - rise. _____ Let God a - rise. _____ Our God

reigns now and for-ev - er. He reigns now and for-ev - er.

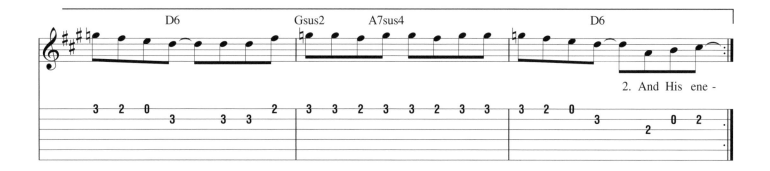

2. And His ene -

- er. God a - rise. _____ Let God a - rise. _____ Our God reigns now and for-ev-

13

*Let chords ring, next 8 meas.

Additional Lyrics

2. And His enemies will run for sure.
   The church will stand, she will endure.
   He holds the keys of life, our Lord.
   Death has no sting, no final word.

Everlasting God

Words and Music by Brenton Brown and Ken Riley

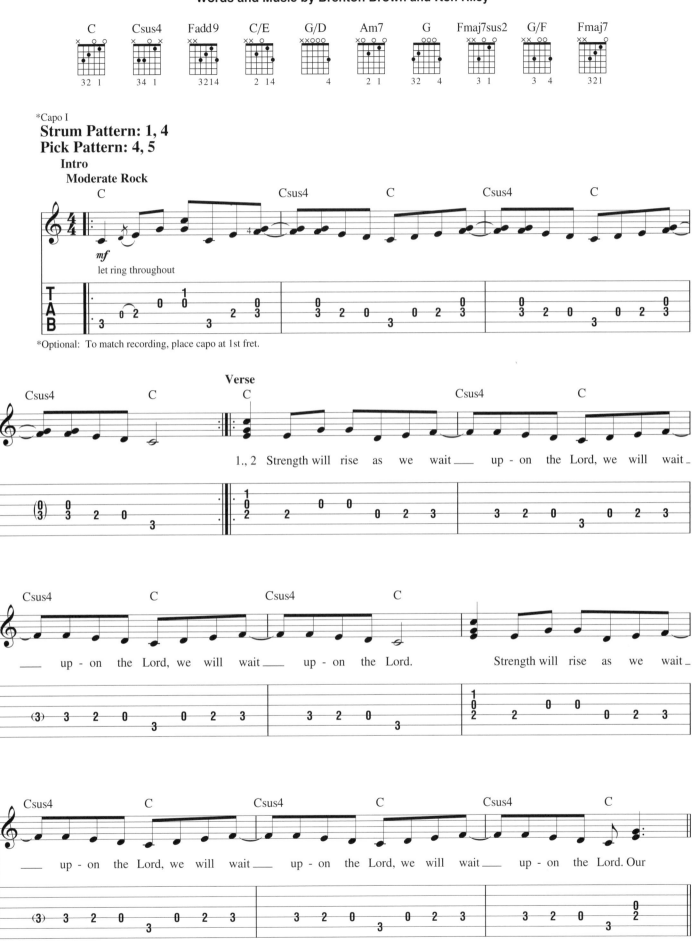

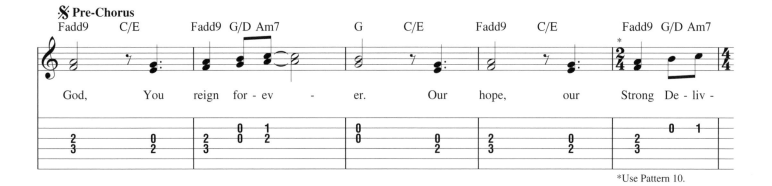

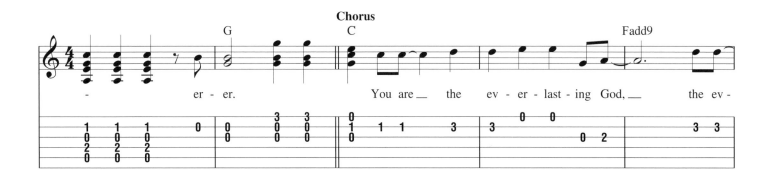

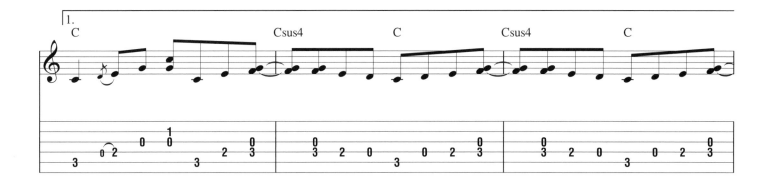

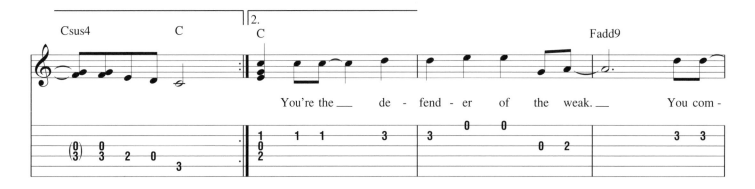

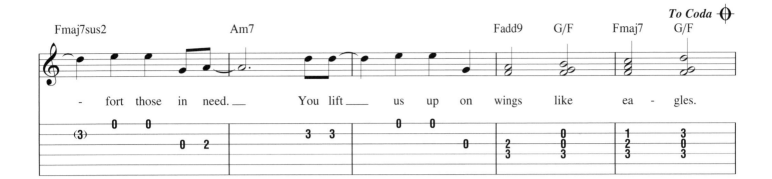

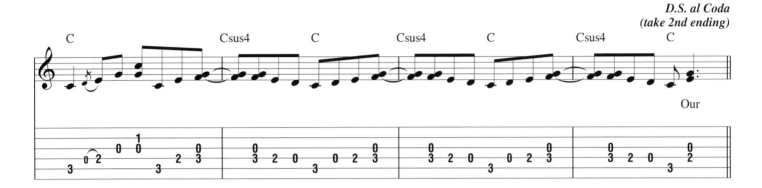

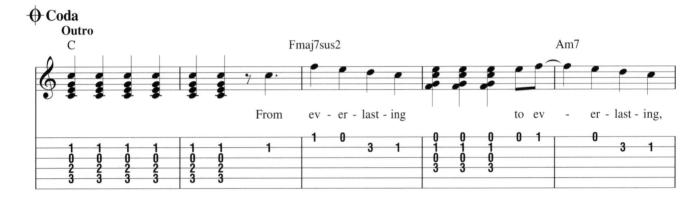

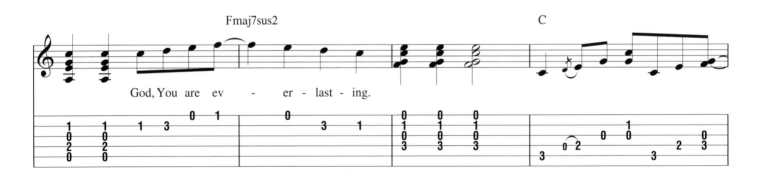

Glory in the Highest

Words and Music by Chris Tomlin, Jesse Reeves, Daniel Carson, Matt Redman and Ed Cash

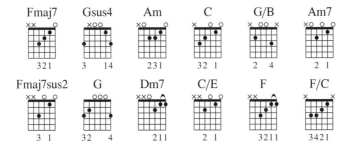

Strum Pattern: 3
Pick Pattern: 1, 6

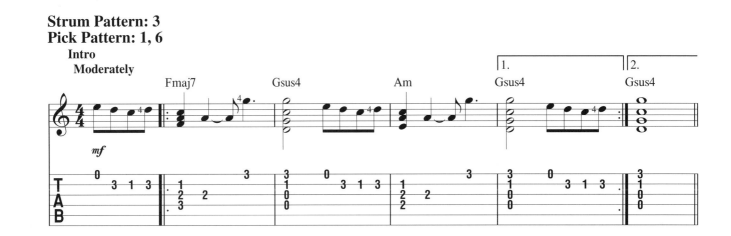

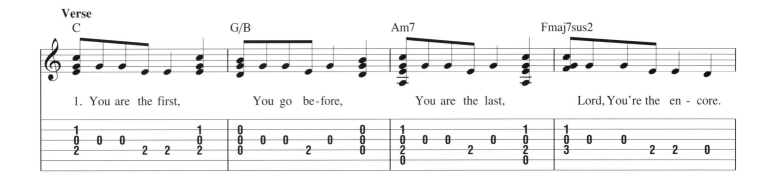

1. You are the first,   You go be-fore,   You are the last,   Lord, You're the en - core.

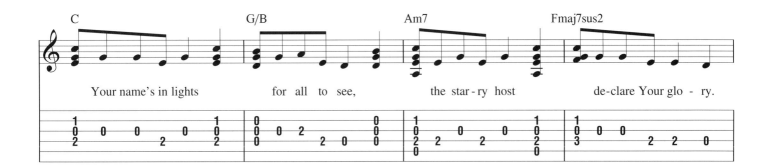

Your name's in lights   for all to see,   the star - ry host   de-clare Your glo - ry.

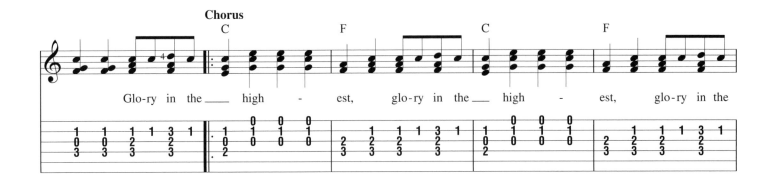

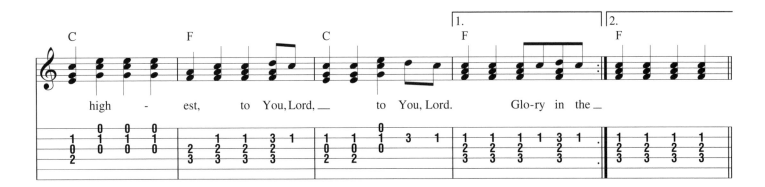

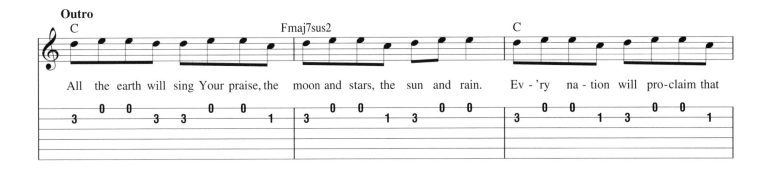

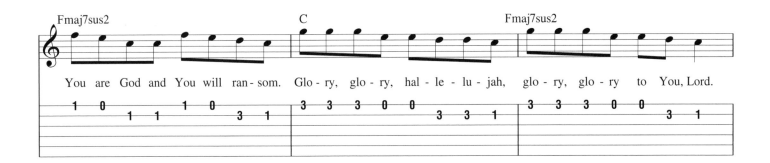

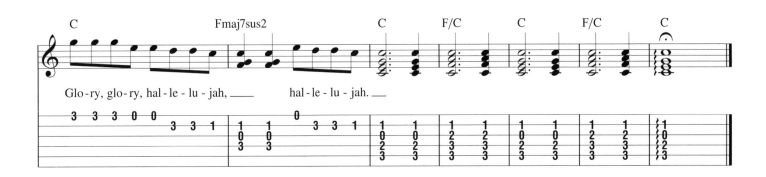

Glorious

Words and Music by Chris Tomlin and Jesse Reeves

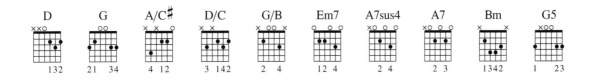

Strum Pattern: 1
Pick Pattern: 1

Intro
Moderately

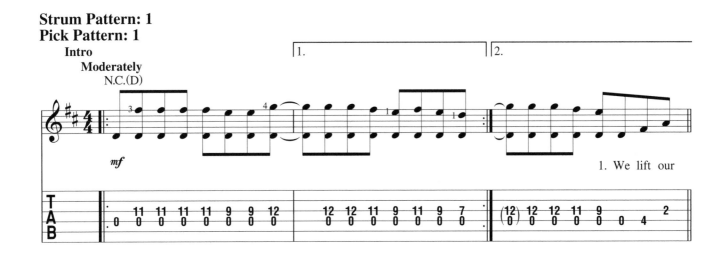

1. We lift our

Verse

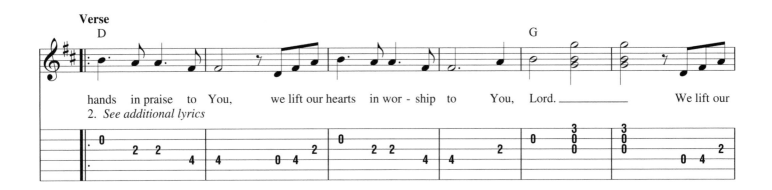

hands in praise to You, we lift our hearts in wor - ship to You, Lord. _____ We lift our
2. *See additional lyrics*

voice to You and sing, our great-est love will ev - er be You, Lord, _____ You, Lord.

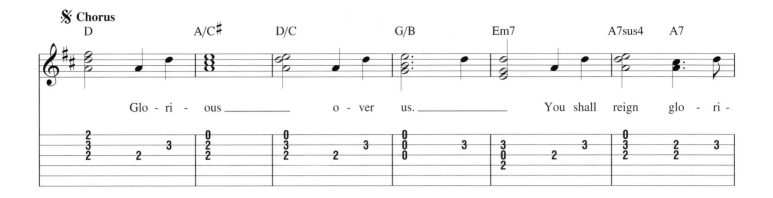

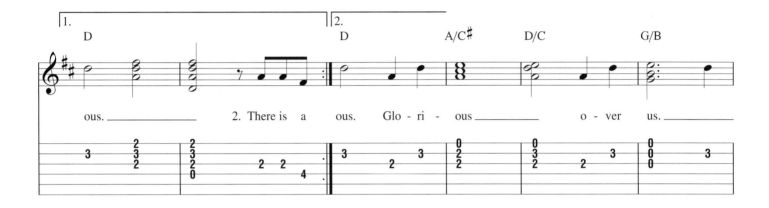

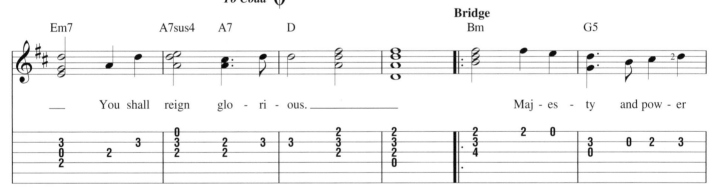

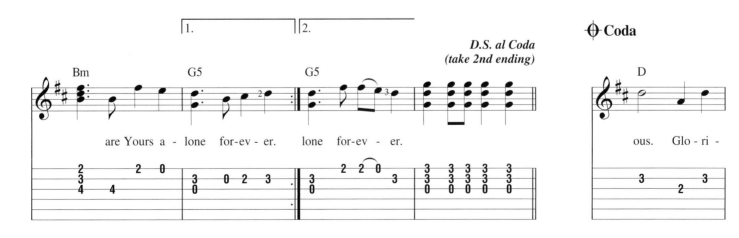

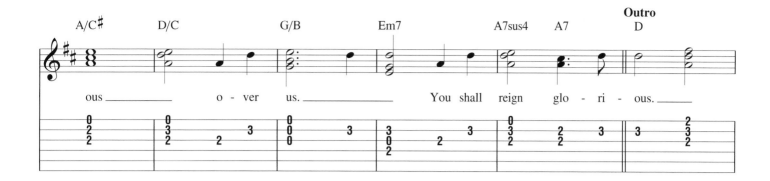

ous _____ o - ver us. _____ You shall reign glo - ri - ous. _____

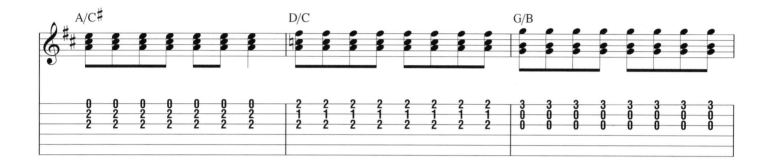

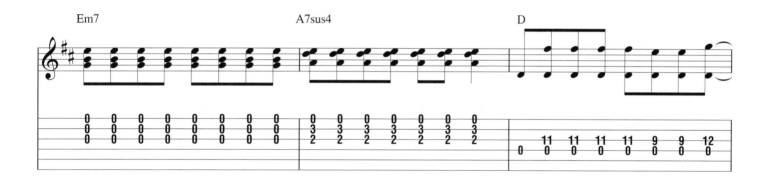

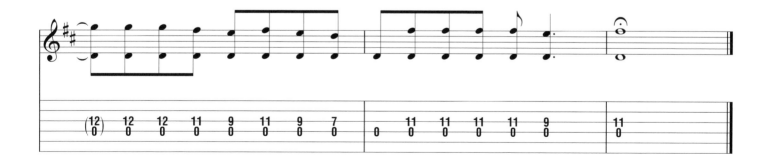

Additional Lyrics

2. There is a King that we adore.
   With humble hearts we bow before You, Lord.
   There is a place we long to be.
   Face to face, we long to see You, Lord, You, Lord.

Awesome Is the Lord Most High

Words and Music by Chris Tomlin, Jesse Reeves, Cary Pierce and Jon Abel

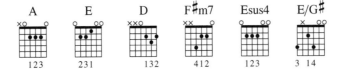

Strum Pattern: 1, 5
Pick Pattern: 1, 2

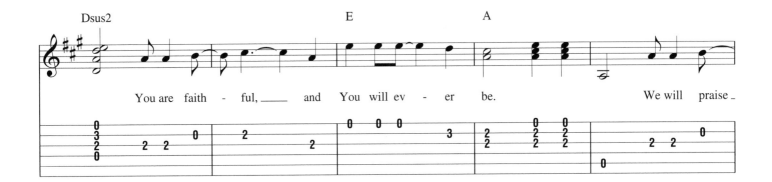

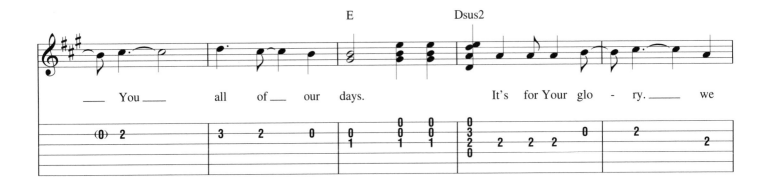

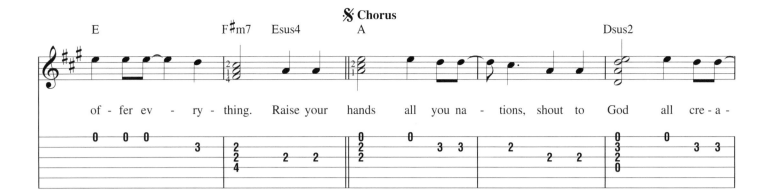

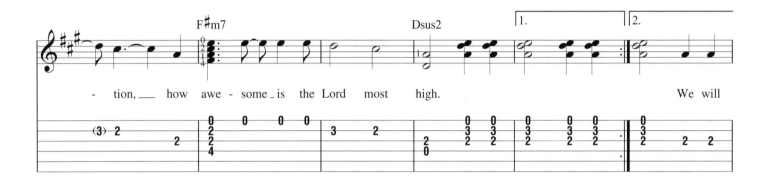

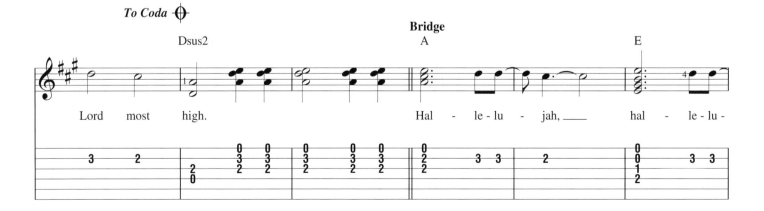

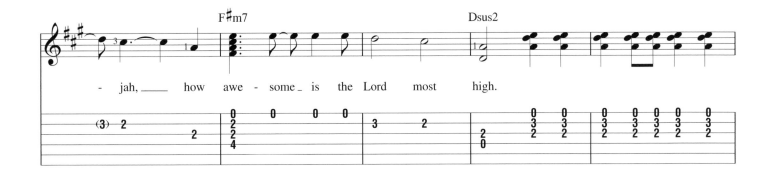

D.S. al Coda
(take 2nd ending)

⊕ Coda

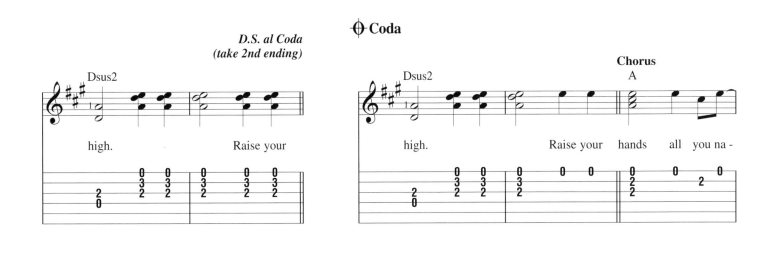

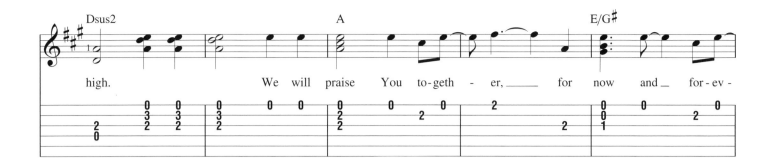

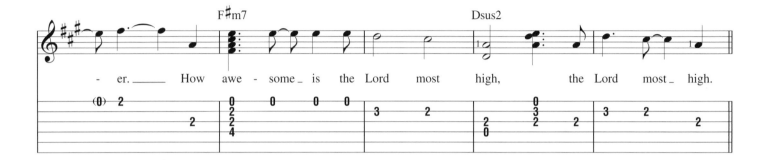

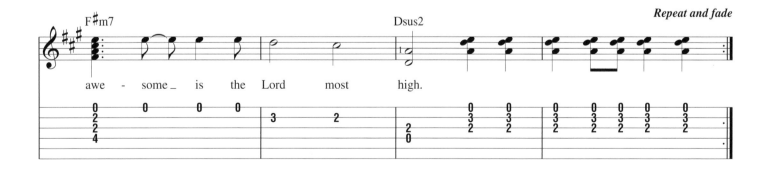

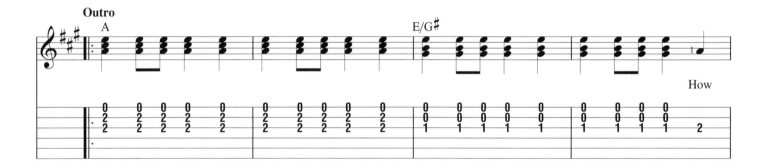

Additional Lyrics

2. Where You send us, God we will go.
   You're the answer, we want the world to know.
   We will trust You when You call our name.
   Where You lead us, we'll follow all the way.

Rejoice

Words and Music by Chris Tomlin, Jesse Reeves and Ed Cash

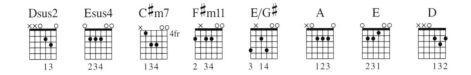

Strum Pattern: 7, 8
Pick Pattern: 7, 8

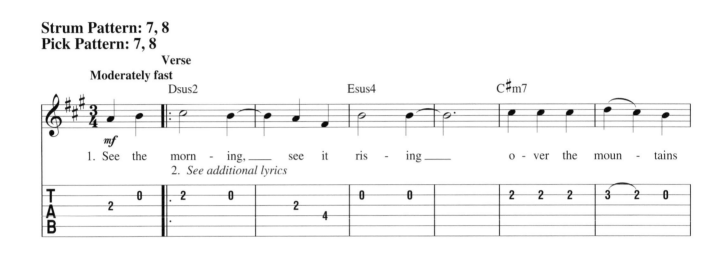

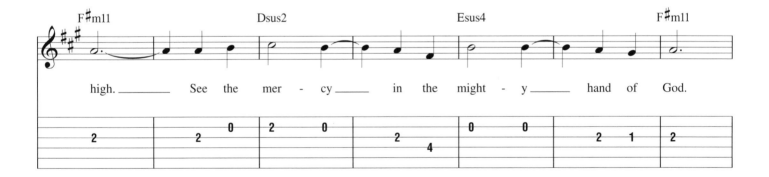

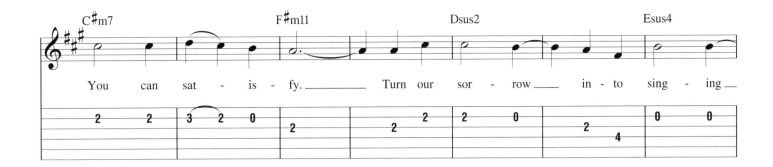

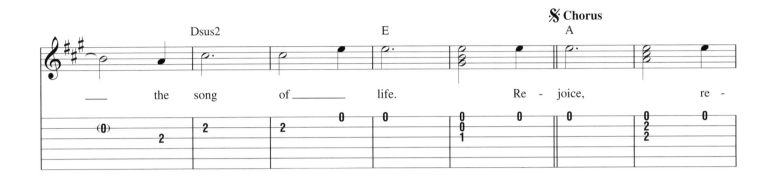

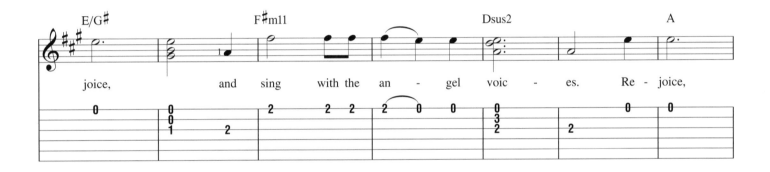

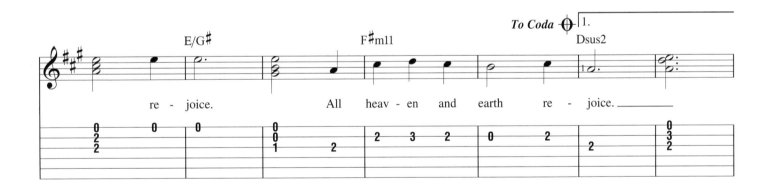

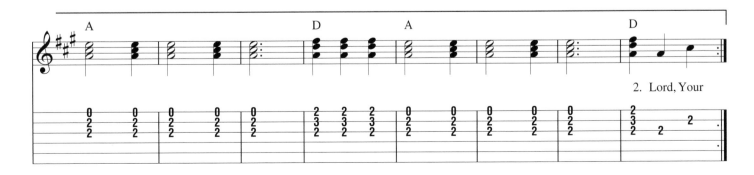

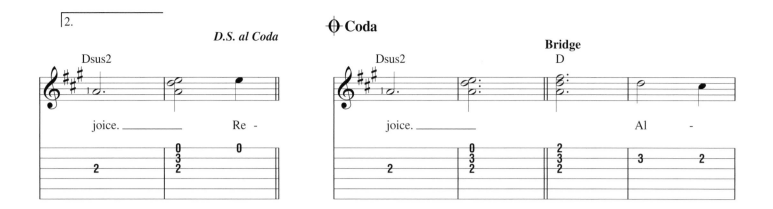

D.S. al Coda

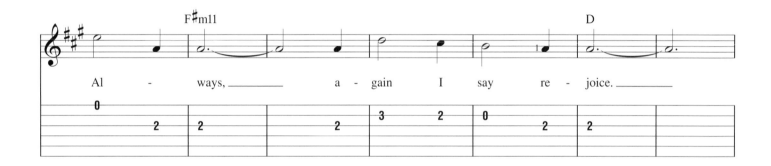

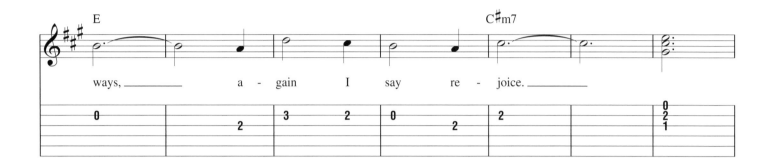

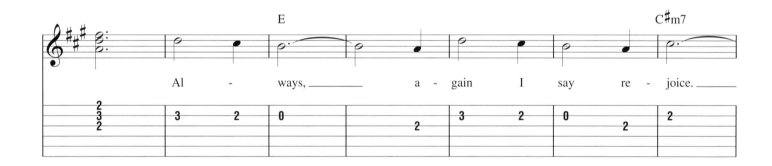

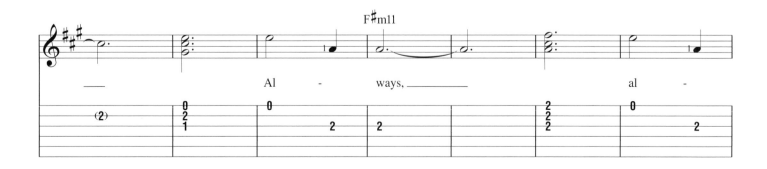

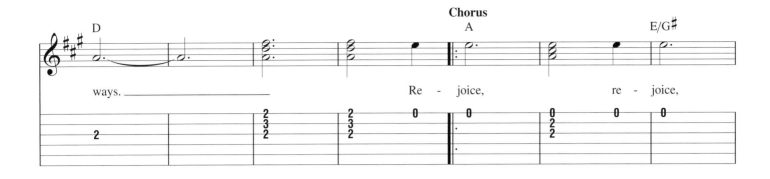

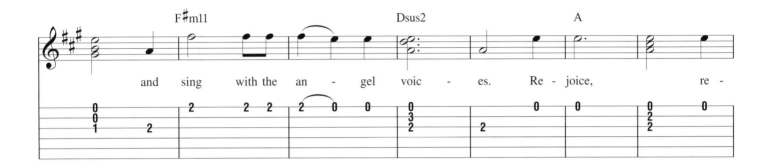

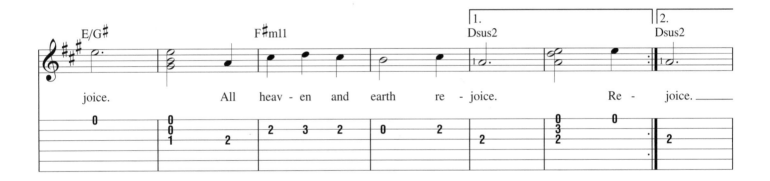

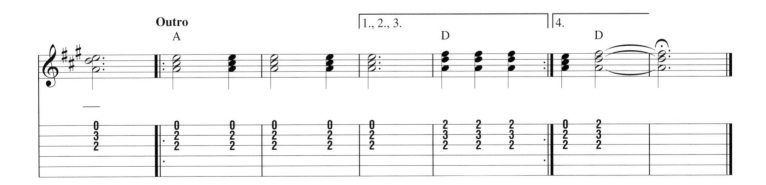

Additional Lyrics

2. Lord, Your strength is like a tower
   The righteous run into.
   Lord, Your love is a banner over us.
   And we hold on to the promise
   That Your hold on us is true.
   There's no other like You, Jesus.
   No one like You.

Let Your Mercy Rain

Words and Music by Chris Tomlin, Jesse Reeves and Ed Cash

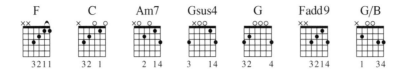

Strum Pattern: 1, 3
Pick Pattern: 4, 5

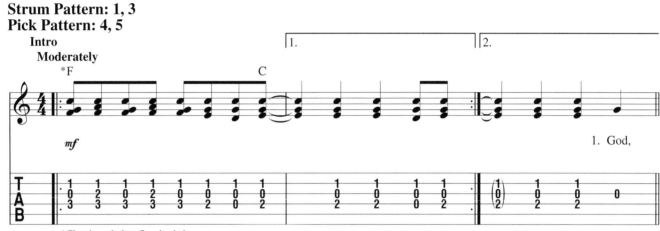

*Chord symbols reflect basic harmony.

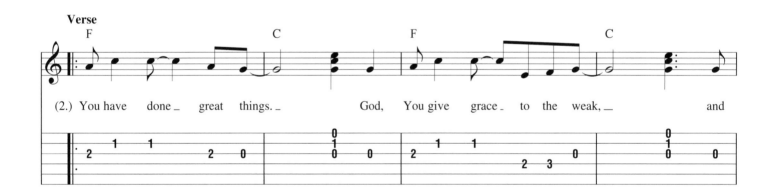

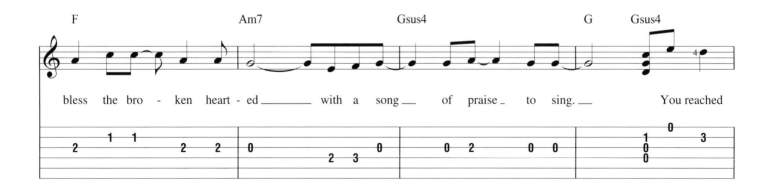

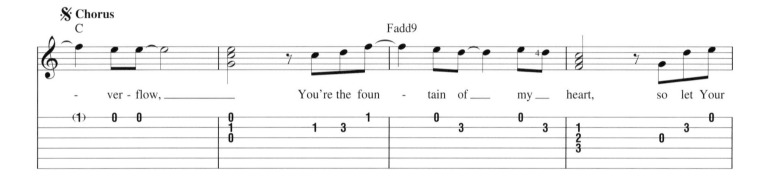

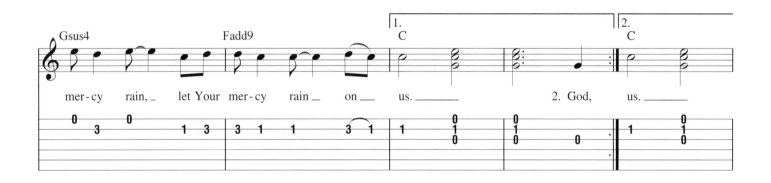

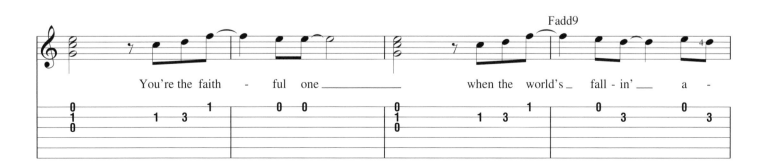

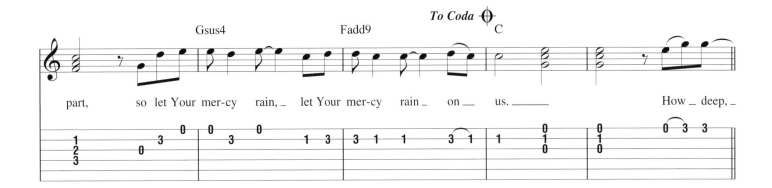

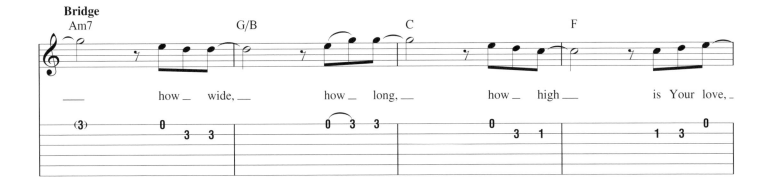

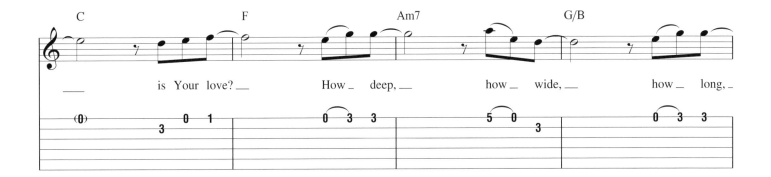

𝕆 **Coda**

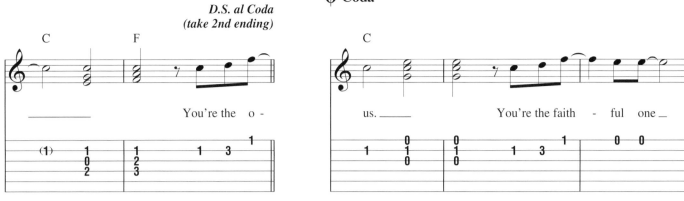

You're the o-

You're the faith - ful one —

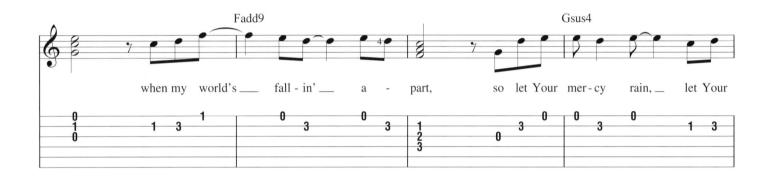

when my world's ___ fall - in' ___ a - part,   so let Your mer - cy   rain, __ let Your

Outro

mer - cy   rain _____   on ___   us.

*Let chord ring.

Repeat and fade

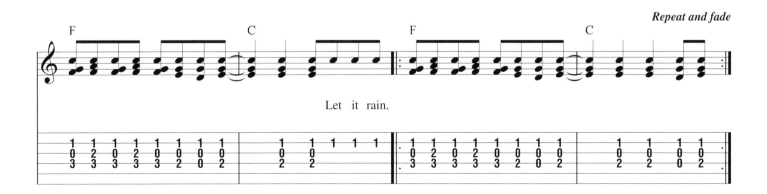

Let it rain.

Amazing Grace
(My Chains Are Gone)

Words by John Newton
Traditional American Melody

Additional Words and Music by Chris Tomlin and Louie Giglio

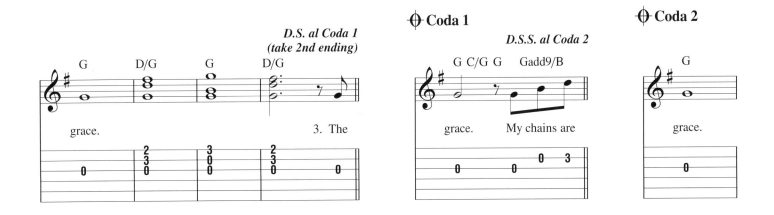

Coda 1

Coda 2

D.S. al Coda 1
(take 2nd ending)

D.S.S. al Coda 2

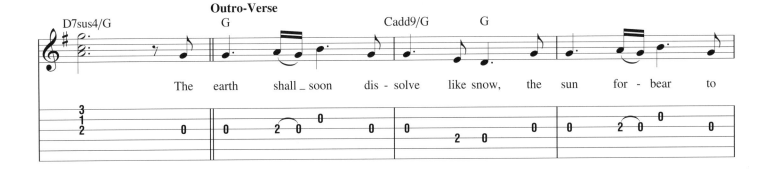

Outro-Verse

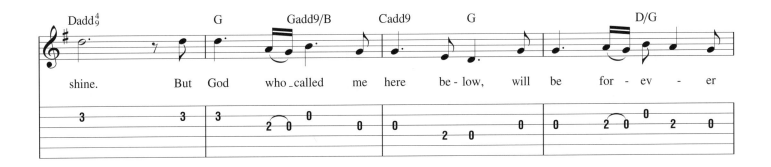

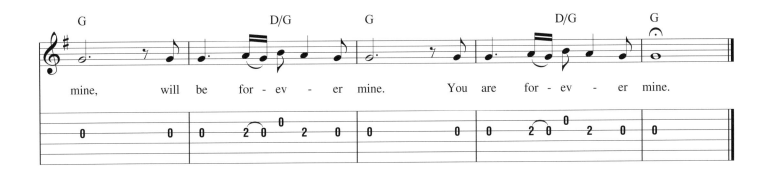

Additional Lyrics

2. 'Twas grace that taught my heart to fear,
   And grace my fears relieved.
   How precious did that grace appear
   The hour I first believed.

3. The Lord has promised good to me.
   His word my hope secures.
   He will my shield and portion be,
   As long as life endures.

Uncreated One

Words and Music by Chris Tomlin and J.D. Walt

*Capo I

Strum Pattern: 2
Pick Pattern: 2

Intro
Moderately slow

mf
w/ fingers
let ring throughout

*Optional: To match recording, place capo at 1st fret.

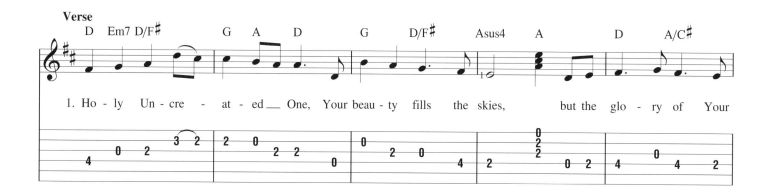

1. Ho - ly Un - cre - at - ed __ One, Your beau - ty fills the skies, but the glo - ry of Your

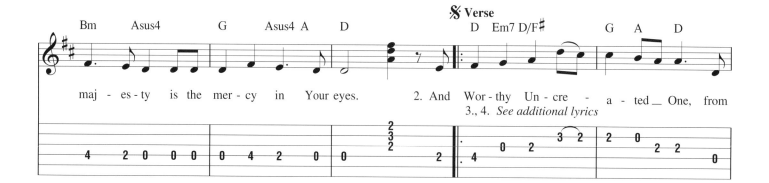

maj - es - ty is the mer - cy in Your eyes.

2. And Wor - thy Un - cre - a - ted __ One, from
3., 4. *See additional lyrics*

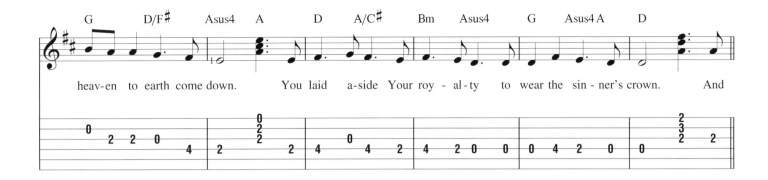

heav-en to earth come down. You laid a-side Your roy - al-ty to wear the sin - ner's crown. And

Chorus

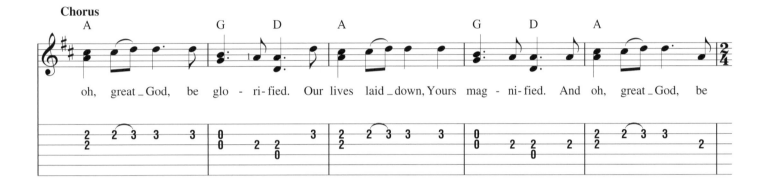

oh, great _ God, be glo - ri-fied. Our lives laid _ down, Yours mag - ni-fied. And oh, great _ God, be

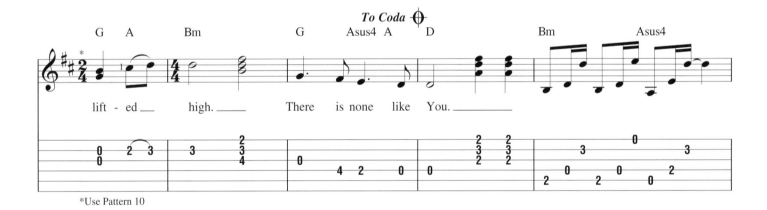

lift - ed _ high. _ There is none like You. _

*Use Pattern 10

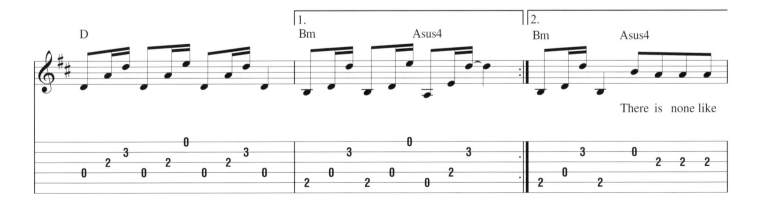

There is none like

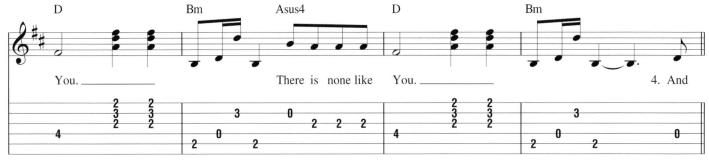

You._____ There is none like You._____ 4. And

Coda

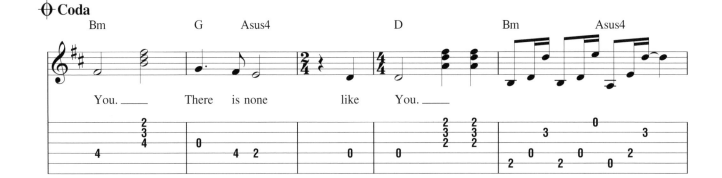

You.____ There is none like You.____

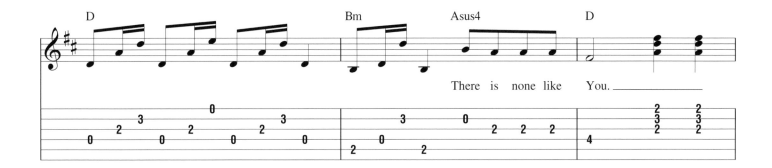

There is none like You._____

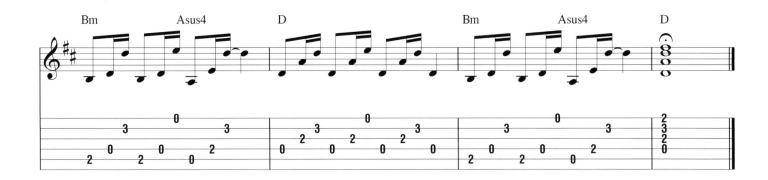

Additional Lyrics

3. Jesus, Savior, God's own Son,
   Risen reigning Lord.
   Sustainer of the universe
   By the power of Your Word.

4. And when we see Your matchless face,
   In speechless awe we'll stand.
   And there we'll bow with grateful hearts
   Unto the great I Am.